LEILA FLETCHER
PRIMER

'Lets Begin'

Musical discovery for young beginners

by Debra Wanless

ISBN 0-921965-29-X

Copyright © 2005 by Mayfair Montgomery Publishing (Div. JAL Holdings Ltd)
203 - 2600 John Street, Markham Ontario Canada L3R 3W3
All Rights Reserved . Printed in Canada

www.leilafletcher.com

PREFACE

The Primer provides a preparatory book for the Leila Fletcher Piano Course and is a wonderful companion to book one. It has been written to answer the demand for a non-staff edition for young students. The Leila Fletcher Primer develop's keyboard exploration, musical creativity, aural skills, rhythm concepts, fingering technique and theoretical knowledge. Music basics are introduced at a comfortable rate through tuneful and child friendly melodies.

The study of music should be a delightful experience This primer continues in the Leila Fletcher tradition of the ability to read music fluently and intrepret it artistically, the establishing of a sound and comprehensive piano technique, the nuturing of the creative musical talent and the fostering of a lasting appreciation of music.

Author Debra Wanless is principal of the Canadian National Conservatory of Music, and is an active examiner, clinician and festival adjudicator. Debra is a pedagogy specialist whose students have earned the Cora B. Arhens award for pedagogy excellence. She is the recipient of the ORMTA Special Teachers Award and has received a Certificate of Merit from the Dictionary of International Biography, Cambridge, England. Debra has authored over twenty educational piano editions.

THE BEST WAY TO USE THIS PRIMER

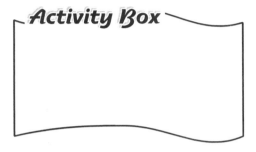

Activity Box

Activity Boxes should be prepared during the lesson and practised daily at home by the student.

Listening Game

Listening Games should be done at lessons but families are encouraged to play these games at home with the student.

Students should sing along with every song.

Practise Balloons: Students should color in or place a check mark ✓ in a balloon for each day the page was practised.

DISCOVERING PIANO SOUNDS

Hi! My Name is Max!

I love to play the piano.

We are going to have fun learning to play the piano together.

The piano is a wonderful musical instrument.

The piano can make loud sounds and soft sounds.

The piano can make high sounds and low sounds.

The piano can sound like a tiny bird, and it can also sound like a thunderstorm.

Activity Box

1. Make loud sounds on the piano. Make soft sounds on the piano.
2. Find the high sounds on the piano. Find the low sounds.
3. Make some tiny bird sounds. Make some thunderstorm sounds.

EXPLORING THE PIANO

Pianos come in many shapes, sizes and colors.

| Grand Piano | Upright Piano | Electronic Piano |

It takes many parts of the piano to make all of the different sounds.
Some of these parts are called hammers, strings, keys and pedals.

Activity Box

1. Have your teacher help you look inside the piano. Touch the strings and feel the soft hammers.
2. Play one key and then play the same key again with one of the pedals pressed down. How did the sound change ?
3. Color the piano that looks most like yours.

POSTURE CHECK

Now that you know how to make a sound on the piano, it is time to learn how to sit at the piano.

Activity Box

Posture Check List

1. ☐ Sit tall with a straight back, but don't be stiff.

2. ☐ Sit near the edge of the piano bench that is closest to the keys.

3. ☐ The bench may also need to be moved. Stretch your arms out straight and with your knuckles touch the wooden part of the piano just above the keys. This will help you sit the right distance from the piano.

4. ☐ Feet should be flat on the floor or use a stool to support your feet.

5. ☐ Shoulders, arms, wrists and hands should feel relaxed.

6. ☐ Lift your arms to the keyboard and make a relaxed but straight line with the forearm and wrist. Let your fingers relax and curve.

FINGER WIGGLE

Your hands and fingers will also need some special attention.

Activity Box

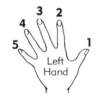

Left Hand

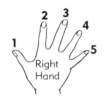

Right Hand

Finger Wiggle

Hold your hands out in front of you
and do the *Finger Wiggle!*

1. Wiggle Mr. Tommy Thumb, *(Wiggle your thumbs)*
He is finger number 1

2. Peter Pointer points for you, *(Shake your pointer finger)*
We will call him finger 2

3. Middle finger, tall and free, *(wiggle your middle finger)*
This is called finger 3

4. If we add just one more, *(wiggle finger number four)*
Now we have finger 4

5. Smallest finger, dip and dive *(wiggle your little finger)*
Baby's name is finger 5

6. One, two, three, four, five, *(wiggle the correct finger number)*
Five, four, three, two, one,
Four, two, three, five, one
Finger wiggle now is done!

ACTIVITY PAGE

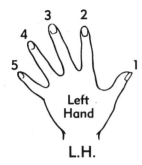

L.H.

Place your hands on this page and
have your teacher trace both hands.

Label your right hand and left hand.
Number each finger correctly.

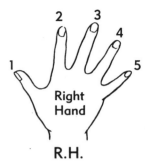

R.H.

KEYBOARD ADVENTURE

The piano keyboard has black and white keys.

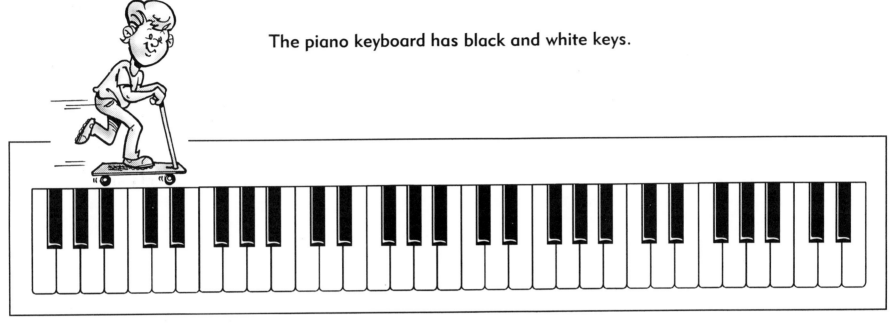

Low Sounds   High Sounds

Activity Box

1. On the keyboard play a song with only high notes.

2. On the keyboard make up a song with only low notes.

3. On the keyboard, use only the black notes and make up a song that uses both high and low sounds.

4. Give each of your songs a title.

EXPLORING THE BLACK KEYS

The black keys are grouped in 2's or twins and 3's or triplets

Activity Box

Start on the lowest set of twins on your piano and play every set until you reach the highest twins.

How many sets of twins did you play? _____

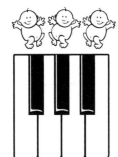

Activity Box

Start on the highest group of triplets on your piano and play every group until you reach the lowest triplets.

How many groups of triplets did you play? _____

ACTIVITY PAGE

You will need to get your hands and fingers into shape and ready to play!

Activity Box

1. Stand up and let your arms hang and relax at your sides.

2. Let your hands and fingers relax too!

3. Notice the relaxed curves in your fingers.
   This is the perfect shape for playing the piano!

Activity Box

1. Sit at a table.

2. Place your forearm and hand flat on the table.
   Remember to stay relaxed!

3. Keep your arm and wrist relaxed on the table.
   Slowly pull up your fingers until they are sitting on their fingertips.

4. Say the *Finger Wiggle* and tap each finger on the table top.

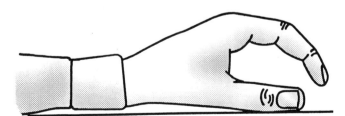

BIG FOOT

Big Foot uses only the black key twins.
Fingers 2 and 3 will play the twins at the same time.

Your right hand starts on the highest twins and moves down the keyboard to the lowest twins.

R.H.
3
2
Big

3
2
Foot

3
2
stomp-

3
2
in'

3
2
down

3
2
the

3
2
path.

Your left hand starts on the lowest twins and moves up the keyboard.

L.H.
2
3
Great

2
3
big

2
3
feet

2
3
and

2
3
fun-

2
3
ny

2
3
laugh.

Color in a balloon, or put in a ✔ every time you do this page, (completing 6 times should make you a superstar).

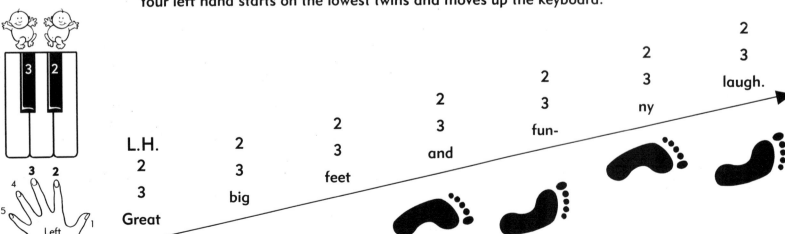

DUCKS

Ducks use only the black key twins to make a quacking sound. Fingers 2 and 3 will play the twins at the same time.

Your right hand starts on the highest twins and moves down and up on the keyboard.

Listening Game

Teacher or Student:
Plays high or low "Quacks" on the twins.

Student or Teacher:
Without looking identify the "Quacks" as high or low.

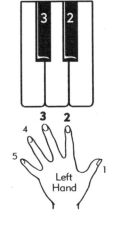

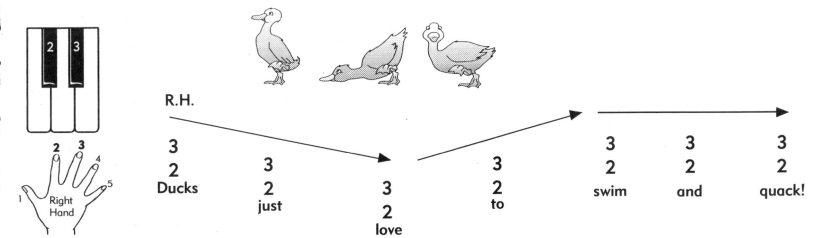

R.H.

3 2 Ducks	3 2 just	3 2 love	3 2 to	3 2 swim	3 2 and	3 2 quack!

Your left hand starts on the lowest twins and moves up and down the keyboard.

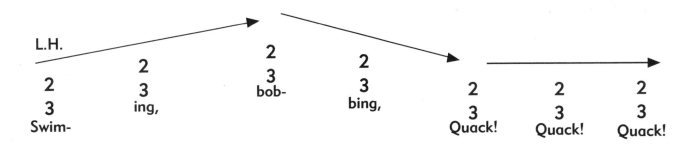

L.H.

2 3 Swim-	2 3 ing,	2 3 bob-	2 3 bing,	2 3 Quack!	2 3 Quack!	2 3 Quack!

Color in a balloon, or put in a ✔ every time you do this page, (completing 6 times should make you a superstar).

THE BIG PARADE

The Big Parade uses only the black twins.

Fingers 2 and 3 will play the twins at the same time.

Your left hand and right hand takes turns playing the twins up and down the keyboard.

L.H.   R.H.

2 3   3 2

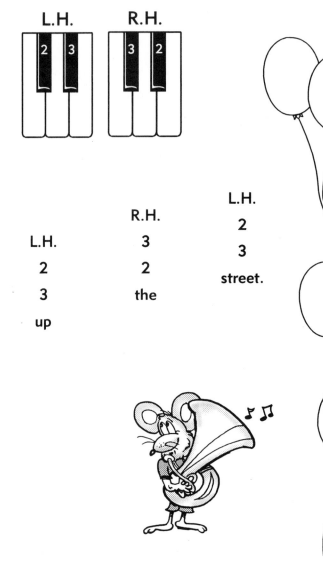

L.H. (left hand) starts on the lowest twins.

R.H. (right hand) starts on the highest twins.

L.H.
3 2
4
5   1
Left
Hand

2 3
1   4
      5
Right
Hand

L.H.
2
3
Left,

R.H.
3
2
Bands

R.H.
3
2
3
Right,

L.H.
2
3
and

L.H.
2
3
march-

R.H.
3
2
clowns

R.H.
3
2
ing

L.H.
2
3
and

L.H.
2
3
up

R.H.
3
2
stomp-

L.H.
2
3
the

R.H.
3
2
ing

L.H.
2
3
street.

L.H.
2
3
feet.

R.H.
3
2

Color in a balloon, or put in a ✓ every time you do this page, (completing 6 times should make you a superstar).

ROCK CLIMBING

Rock Climbing uses only the black key twins.

Fingers 2 and 3 will play the twins.

When the numbers are side by side play the twins one after the other.

L.H. (left hand) starts on the lowest twins.

Your left hand and right hand take turns playing the twins.

On the second line, the R.H. starts on the highest twins.

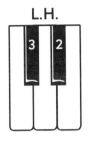

L.H.   R.H.

L. H.
3   2

Left Hand,

R. H.
2   3

Right Hand,

L. H.
3   2

high-er,

R. H.
2   3

high-er,

L. H.
3   2

up the

R. H.
2   3

rock face

L. H.
2
3

wall!

R. H.
3   2

Right Hand,

L. H.
2   3

Left Hand,

R. H.
3   2

low-er,

L. H.
2   3

low-er,

R. H.
3   2

make sure,

L. H.
2   3

you don't,

R. H.
3
2

fall!

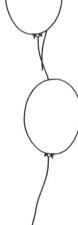

Color in a balloon, or put in a ✔ every time you do this page, (completing 6 times should make you a superstar).

DINOSAUR STOMP

Dinosaur Stomp uses only the black key triplets.

Fingers 2, 3 and 4 will play the triplets.

When the numbers are side by side play triplets one after the other.

When the numbers are one above the other play the triplets together.

Your left hand and right hand take turns playing the triplets.

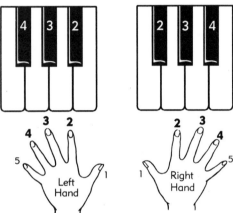

L.H.
Starts on the
lowest triplets.

R.H.
4
3
2
stomp!

L.H.
4   3   2
Din - o - saur

R.H.
4
3
2
stomp!

L.H.
4   3   2
Din - o - saur

R.H.
4
3
2
stomp!

L.H.
4   3   2
Din - o - saur

L.H.
2
3
4
stomp!

Color in a balloon,
or put in a ✓ every
time you do this
page, (completing
6 times should
make you a
superstar).

R.H. starts on the
highest triplets.

R. H –
4 3   2
There he   goes

L. H.
2
3
4
stomp!

R. H.
4 3 2
run-ing fast

Listening Game

Teacher:
1. Choose any set of triplets.
   Show the student which set has been selected.
2. Play the three notes of the triplet consecutively by
   stepping up (ascending) or stepping down (decending).

Student:
1. Listen without looking at the keyboard.
2. Play back the triplets in the same direction as the teacher.

L. H.
2
3
4
stomp!

R. H.
4 3 2
right in-to

L. H.
2 3 4
the mud-dy

R. H.
4
3
2
swamp!

DISCOVERING NOTES AND BEATS

Music is like the ticking of a clock. It needs to have a steady beat.

Activity Box

Listen to the sound of a clock.

What do you hear?_____

Tap your knees with the same steady sound of the clock.

The musical signs that show you the beats are called NOTES. Each note has its own name and beat or count.

Quarter Note

The quarter note is a one beat or one count note

Say "tah" or "one".

Activity Box

Clap and say.

Say:	tah	tah	tah	tah
Say:	one	one	one	one
Say:	walk	walk	walk	walk
Say:	tick	tick	tick	tick

Think of other things to say for the quarter note. Be sure to keep a steady beat.

Say: _____ _____ _____ _____

Color in a balloon, or put in a ✓ every time you do this page, (completing 6 times should make you a superstar).

TAP, TAP, TAP

Tap, Tap, Tap will be played on any set of twins.
Use finger 2 of each hand to play the twins.

The stick or the stem on the quarter note shows which hand to play.

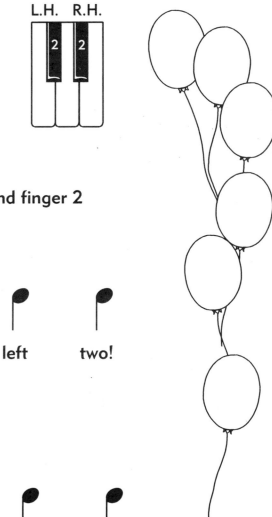

Use the right hand finger 2

Tap,   tap,   right   two!

Tap   right,   Tap   left

Use the left hand finger 2

Tap,   tap   left   two!

Tap   tap,   tap   two!

Color in a balloon, or put in a ✔ every time you do this page, (completing 6 times should make you a superstar).

Activity Box

Play *Tap, Tap, Tap* on different sets of twins.

HALF NOTE DISCOVERY

Half Note

The half note is a two beat or two count note.

Say "one two" or "tah-ah".

Activity Box

Clap and say.

Say:	one	one	one	two
Say:	tah	tah	tah	-	ah
Say:	tick	tick	tick	hold
Say:	walk	walk	walk	wait

Activity Box

On the line below, write the number of beats for each note.

___ ___ ___ ___ ___ ___ ___ ___ ___ ___

On a table top, tap the notes while counting out loud. Be sure to tap with the correct hand.

Color in a balloon, or put in a ✓ every time you do this page, (completing 6 times should make you a superstar).

THE ECHO SONG

21

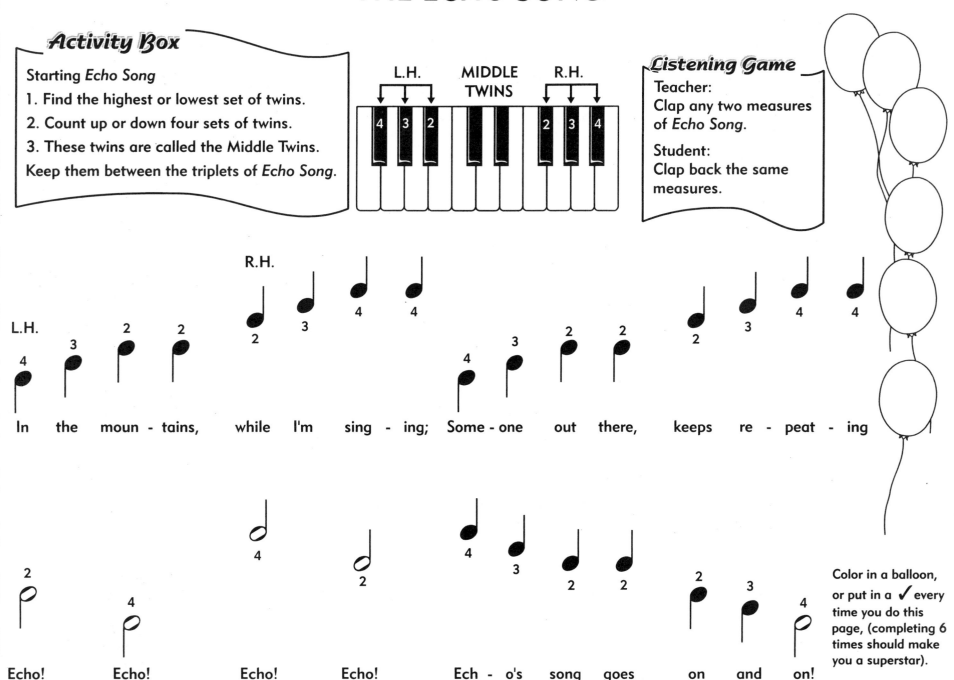

Activity Box

Starting *Echo Song*

1. Find the highest or lowest set of twins.
2. Count up or down four sets of twins.
3. These twins are called the Middle Twins.

Keep them between the triplets of *Echo Song*.

L.H.   MIDDLE TWINS   R.H.

Listening Game

Teacher:
Clap any two measures of *Echo Song*.

Student:
Clap back the same measures.

R.H.

L.H.

In the moun - tains, while I'm sing - ing; Some - one out there, keeps re - peat - ing

Echo! Echo! Echo! Echo! Ech - o's song goes on and on!

Color in a balloon, or put in a ✓ every time you do this page, (completing 6 times should make you a superstar).

AT THE ZOO

L.H. R.H.

R.H. on the middle twins

I see mon - keys, and chim - pan - zes, Li - ons, tig - gers that I fan - cy!

El - e - phants and rhin - os too! I have such fun at the zoo!

Activity Box

Play *At the Zoo* beginning with other sets of twins and triplets.

Accompaniment for teacher or advanced student.

Color in a balloon, or put in a ✓ every time you do this page, (completing 6 times should make you a superstar).

MEET THE MEASURES

Notes in music are grouped in measures.
Each measure is divided by a Bar Line.
The end of the music or song is marked with a Double Bar Line.

Every measure has the same number of counts or beats.

4 counts in
every measure   1 + 1 + 1 + 1   1 + 1 + 1 + 1

2 counts in
every measure   1 + 1   1 + 1

Time Signature

4 = 4 counts in every measure

♩ = quarter note receives 1 count

Time Signature

The Time Signature is placed at the beginning of the piece.
It shows the number of beats or counts in each measure and the kind of note that receives one beat .

24

ACTIVITY PAGE

Below each note write the number of beats or counts.
Count the number of beats for each measure.
Write the number of beats in a measure at the beginning of each line.

**Counts in
each measure**

**Beats or counts
for each note**

Color in a balloon,
or put in a ✓ every
time you do this
page, (completing
6 times should
make you a
superstar).

Activity Box

Clap and count
each line of notes.

THREE SILLY MICE

Activity Box

Posture Check
Before you play *Three Silly Mice* turn back to page 3 and do a *Posture Check!*

Listening Game

Teacher: Play two consecutive notes or the same note twice.
Student: Identify the two notes as "the same" or "different".

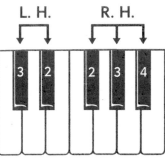

L.H. on the Middle Twins

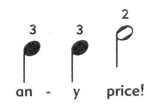

Three Blind Mice!   Sil - ly   Mice!   They   buy cheese at   an - y   price!

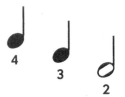

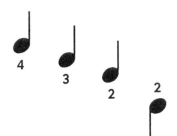
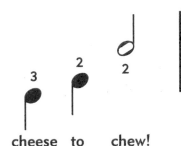

Swiss or   Blue!   White will   do!   Sil - ly mice love   cheese to   chew!

Accompaniment for teacher or advanced student.

1.   2.

Color in a balloon, or put in a ✓ every time you do this page, (completing 6 times should make you a superstar).

OLD MACDONALD

Whole Note

O

The whole note is a four beat or four count note.

Say "1-2-3-4" or "tah-ah-ah-ah"

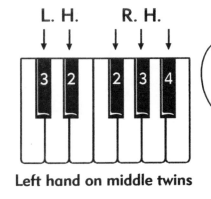

L. H.   R. H.

3 2   2 3 4

Left hand on middle twins

How many counts or beats in each measure?

R.H.

2   2   2
      3

Old   Mac Don - ald   had   a   farm,   E - I - E - I   -   O.

L.H.

2   2   2
      3

On   this farm he   had some ducks,   E - I - E - I   -   O.

Accompaniment for teacher or advanced student.

Fine

D.C. al Fine

Color in a balloon, or put in a ✔ every time you do this page, (completing 6 times should make you a superstar).

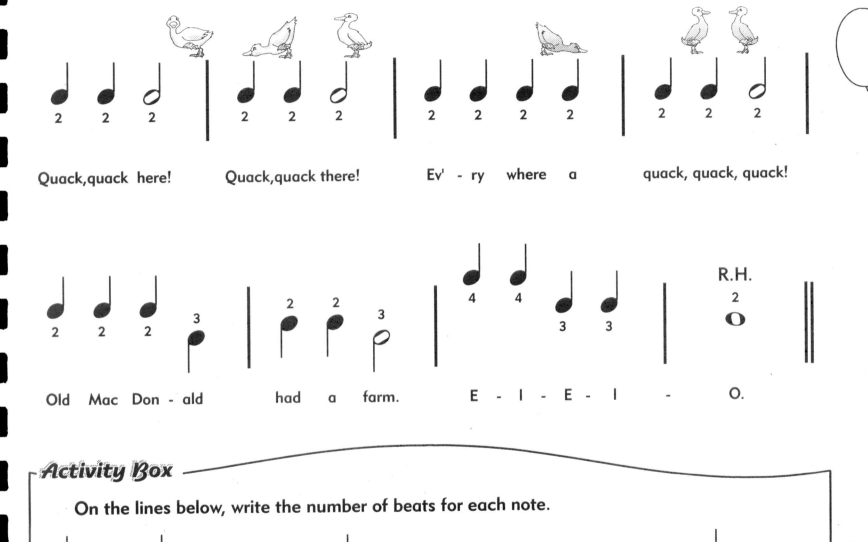

Quack,quack here!   Quack,quack there!   Ev' - ry   where   a   quack, quack, quack!

Old   Mac Don - ald   had   a   farm.   E - I - E - I - O.

Activity Box

On the lines below, write the number of beats for each note.

Color in a balloon, or put in a ✓ every time you do this page, (completing 6 times should make you a superstar).

STAR QUEST

Trace the stars!

Use a blue crayon for the stars with whole notes.

Use a red crayon for the stars with the half notes.

Use a yellow crayon for the stars with quarter notes.

MERRILY WE ROLL ALONG!

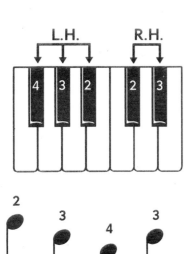

Mer - ri - ly we Roll a - long, Roll a - long Roll a - long!

Mer - ri - ly we roll a - long, O'er the big high - way!

Activity Box

Clap and count the following:

Accompaniment for teacher or advanced student.

Color in a balloon, or put in a ✔ every time you do this page, (completing 6 times should make you a superstar).

29

THE MUSIC ALPHABET

The Music Alphabet has seven letters - A, B, C, D, E, F, G.

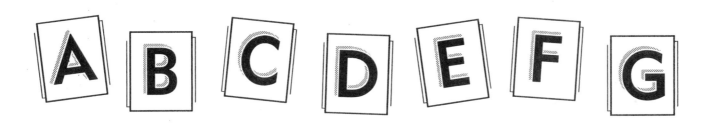

Say the Music Alphabet out loud beginning on the letter A

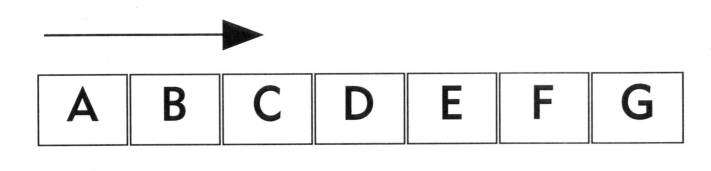

Say the Music Alphabet beginning on the letter G and go backwards to A.

Color in a balloon, or put in a ✔ every time you do this page, (completing 6 times should make you a superstar).

BOOGIE TIME

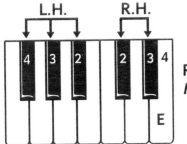

R.H. on the
Middle Twins

The seven letters of the music alphabet are used to name the white keys on the piano.

The white key to the right of the twins is called "E". Find all of the "E's" on the piano.

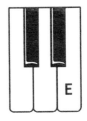

New Note **E**

  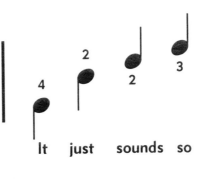 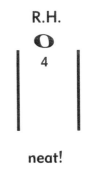

I just love the   boo - gie woo - gie!   It just sounds so   neat!

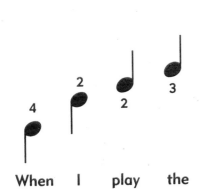    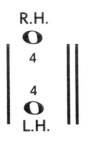

When I play the   boo - gie woo - gie!   I can feel the   beat!

Color in a balloon, or put in a ✔ every time you do this page, (completing 6 times should make you a superstar).

Accompaniment for teacher or advanced student.

THE KEYBOARD AND THE MUSIC ALPHABET

Write the music alphabet.

How many letters are in the music alphabet?_____

These letters are the names for the WHITE keys on the piano keyboard.

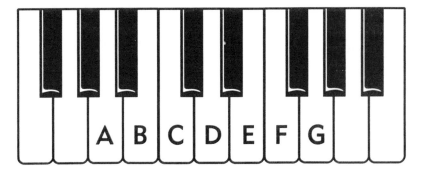

Write the Music Alphabet on the keyboard below.

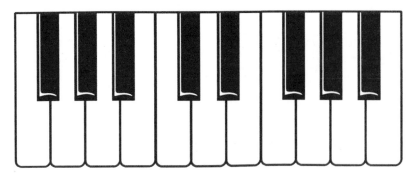

C - D - E

In *Boogie Time!* you played the white key "E".
Now it's time to find "C - D - E".

R.H.

Use finger 2 and 3 of the right hand to find the middle twins.

Let your thumb play the next white key to the left of the twins.

This note uses the letter "C"

R.H.

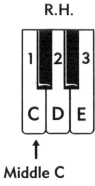

↑
Middle C

This "C" is special because it is beside the Middle Twins and is called Middle C.

Using fingers 1, 2 and 3 of your right hand, play "Middle C - D and E" one after the other.

Activity Box

On the keyboard below color all of the C's red, the D's green and the E's blue.

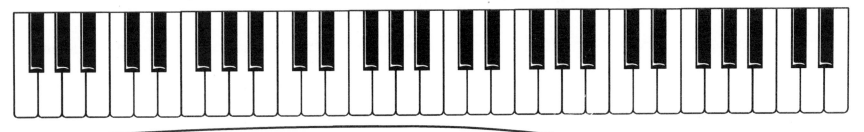

34

THE LOVELY
MERMAID

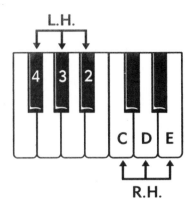

L.H.

4 3 2

C D E

R.H.

4

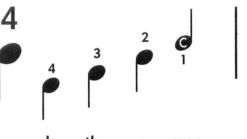 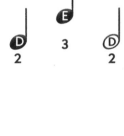 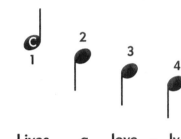 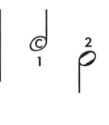

In   the   o - cean   cold   and   blue;   Lives   a   love - ly   mer - maid!

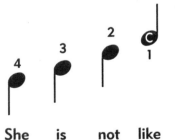 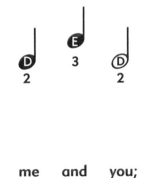 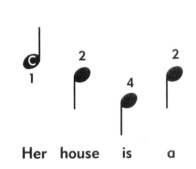 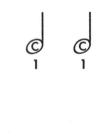

She   is   not   like   me   and   you;   Her   house   is   a   cas - cade!

Activity Box

Pedal Fun

Push down or depress the right pedal with your right foot. Keep your heel on the floor and hold the pedal while you play *The Lovely Mermaid*.

Color in a balloon, or put in a ✔ every time you do this page, (completing 6 times should make you a superstar).

SHARING

The left hand thumb may also play Middle C

Both your right hand thumb and left hand thumb will play middle C in *Sharing*.

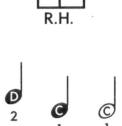

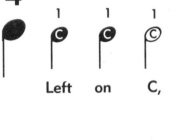 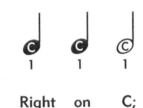 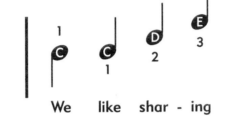 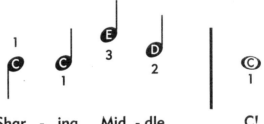 

Left on C,	Right on C;	We like shar - ing	Mid - dle C;

Here we go,	Right once more;	Shar - ing Mid - dle	C!

Accompaniment for teacher or advanced student.

Color in a balloon, or put in a ✔ every time you do this page, (completing 6 times should make you a superstar).

36

A - B - C

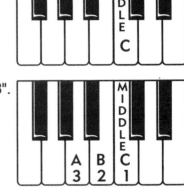

L.H.

Find "Middle C" with your left hand thumb.

Play the note to the left of "Middle C" with finger 2. This note is "B".

Play the note to the left of "B" with finger 3. This note is "A".

Find all of the "A's" on the keyboard and play "A - B - C."

L.H.

Activity Box

Keyboard Fun

On the keyboard below, color all of the A's red, the B's blue, the C's green, the D's yellow and the E's orange.

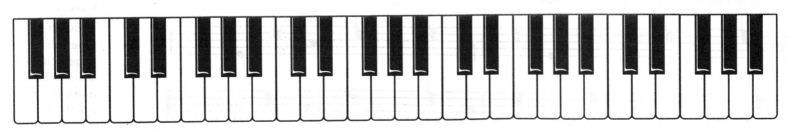

Color in a balloon, or put in a ✔ every time you do this page, (completing 6 times should make you a superstar).

STUCK IN BED!

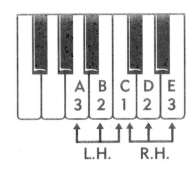

L.H.   R.H.

Activity Box

Time for a *Posture Check!*

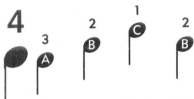 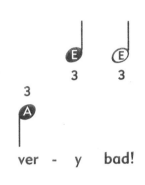  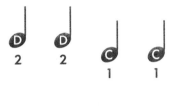 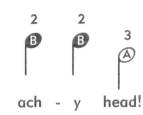 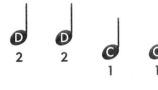 

I   am   feel - ing   ver - y   bad!   Up - set   stom - ach,   ach - y   head!

Now   I'm   sick   and   moth - er   said!   "For   to - day   you're   stuck   in   bed!"

Activity Box

Add Them Up! Add the number of counts for each of the following:

♩ + ♩ = ___   𝅗𝅥 + ♩ = ___   o + o = ___   ♩ + ♪ = ___

𝅗𝅥 + ♪ = ___   𝅗𝅥 + o = ___   o + ♩ = ___   ♩ + ♩ + ♩ = ___

 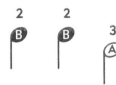

Color in a balloon, or put in a ✓ every time you do this page, (completing 6 times should make you a superstar).

RHYTHM FUN

Dotted Half Note

The dotted half note is a three beat or three count note.

Count "1 - 2 - 3" or "Tah - ah - ah"

Clap and count each line.

3

Tah   tah   tah   tah - ah   tah   tah - ah - ah

4

2

Listening Game

Teacher: Play any of the *Rhythm Fun* measures on the piano. Use repeated notes or create a melody.

Student:
Clap back the measures.

3

Color in a balloon, or put in a ✔ every time you do this page, (completing 6 times should make you a superstar).

SNOWFLAKES

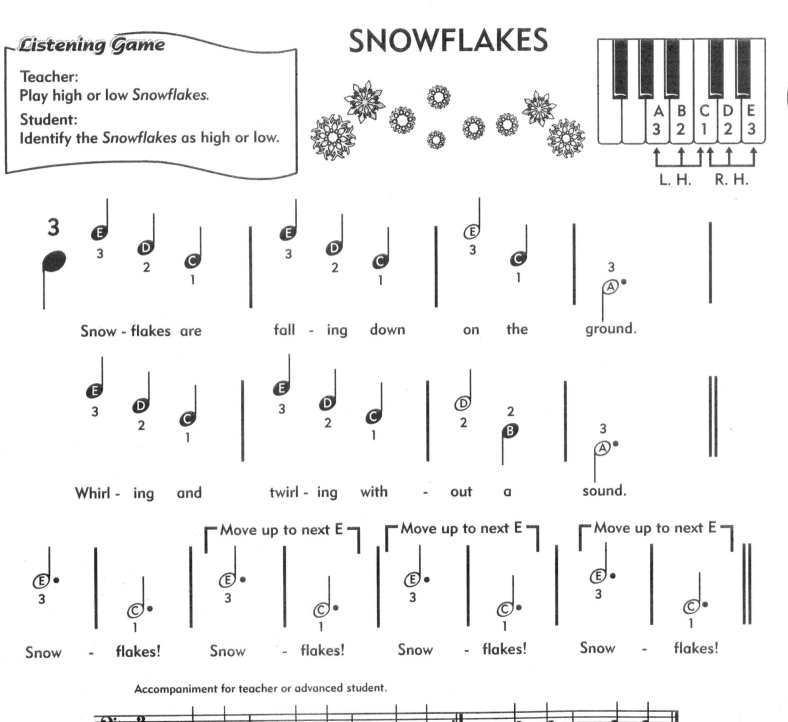

Listening Game

Teacher:
Play high or low *Snowflakes.*

Student:
Identify the *Snowflakes* as high or low.

L. H.   R. H.

3

E3 D2 C1 | E3 D2 C1 | E3 C1 A3 |

Snow - flakes are   fall - ing down   on   the   ground.

E3 D2 C1 | E3 D2 C1 | D2 B2 A3 ‖

Whirl - ing and   twirl - ing with - out a   sound.

⌐Move up to next E⌐ ⌐Move up to next E⌐ ⌐Move up to next E⌐

E3• C1• | E3• C1• | E3• C1• | E3• C1• ‖

Snow - flakes! Snow - flakes! Snow - flakes! Snow - flakes!

Accompaniment for teacher or advanced student.

Color in a balloon, or put in a ✓ every time you do this page, (completing 6 times should make you a superstar).

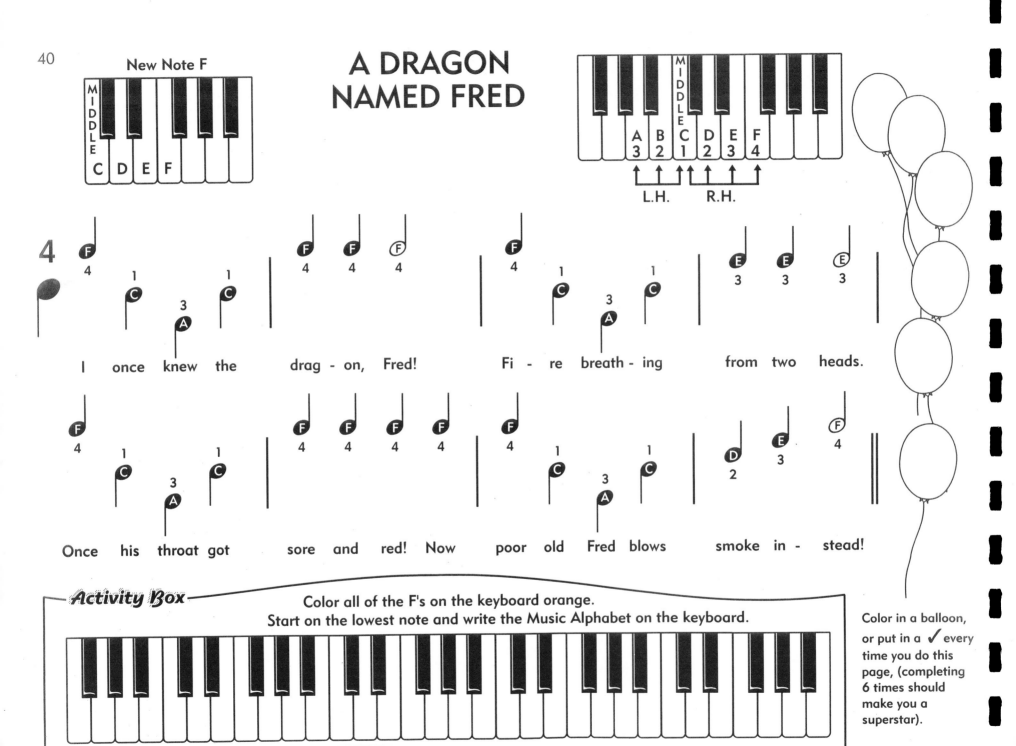

KEYBOARD FUN

On the keyboard color the twins red and the triplets blue.

Start on the lowest white key and print the correct letter name on each key.

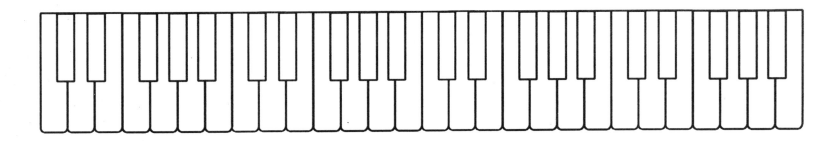

HOW MANY BEATS?

Write the number of counts or beats for each measure.

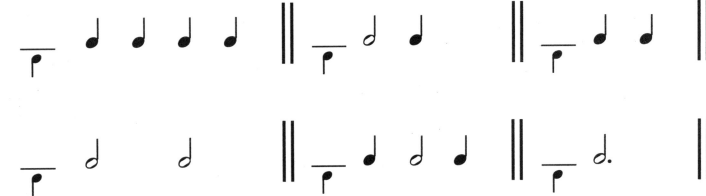

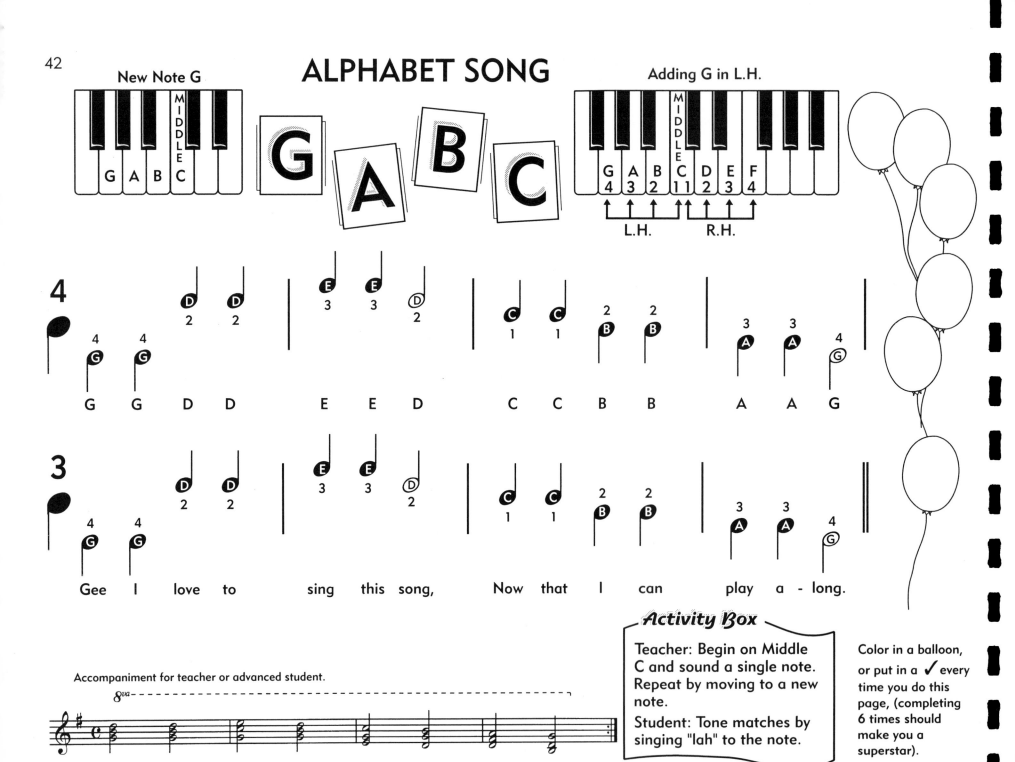

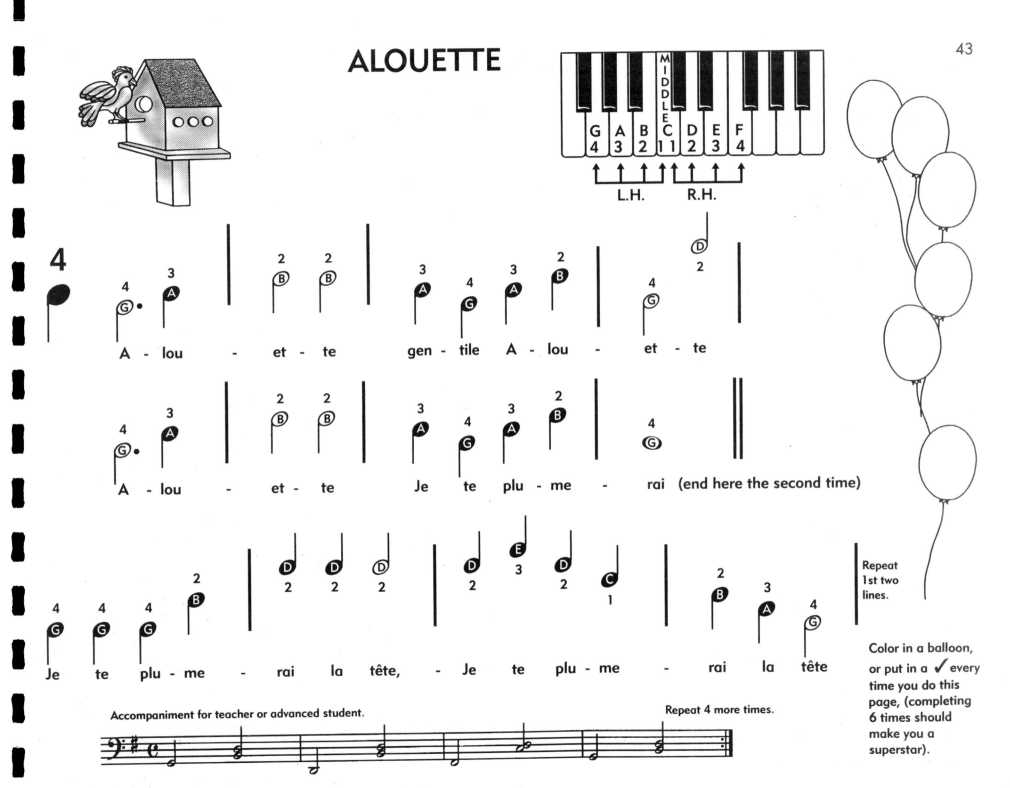

ALOUETTE

44

New Note G

ROYAL
COUNT

Color in a balloon,
or put in a ✓ every
time you do this
page, (completing
6 times should
make you a
superstar).

Activity Box

Play the *Royal Count* use the whole keyboard and play 8 more G's with finger 3.
Let your right hand and left hand take turns playing the G's and count to 8. Repeat the *Royal Count*.

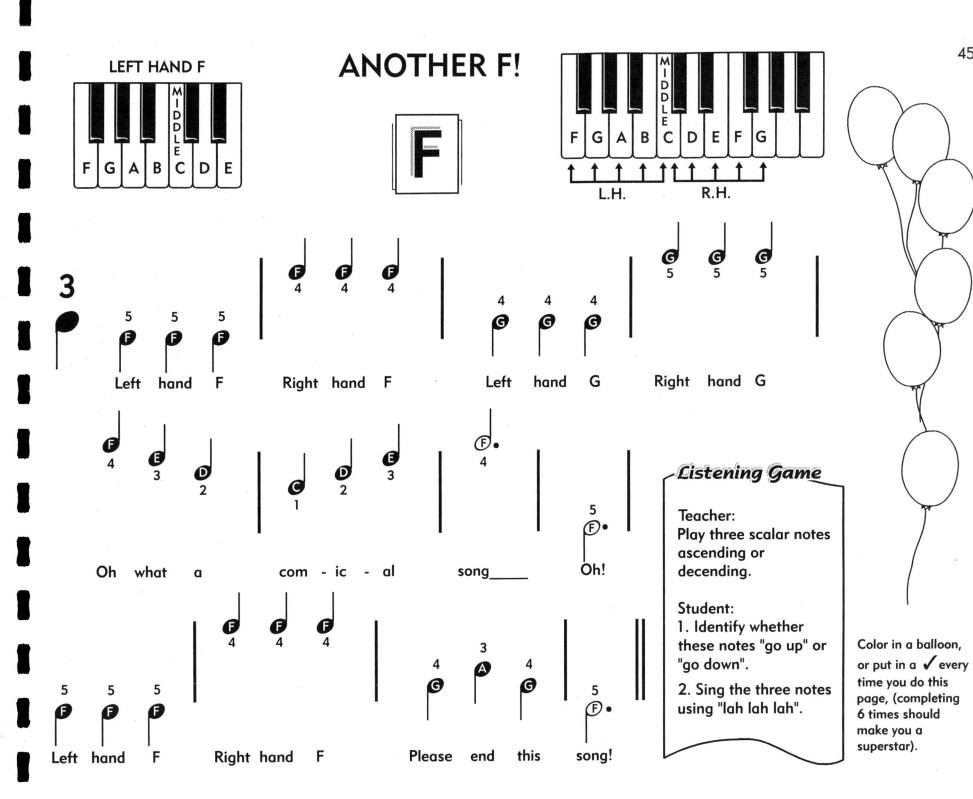

46

Both thumbs share "D"

MOVING DAY

Activity Box

It's time for
a *Finger Wiggle*
and a *Posture Check*.

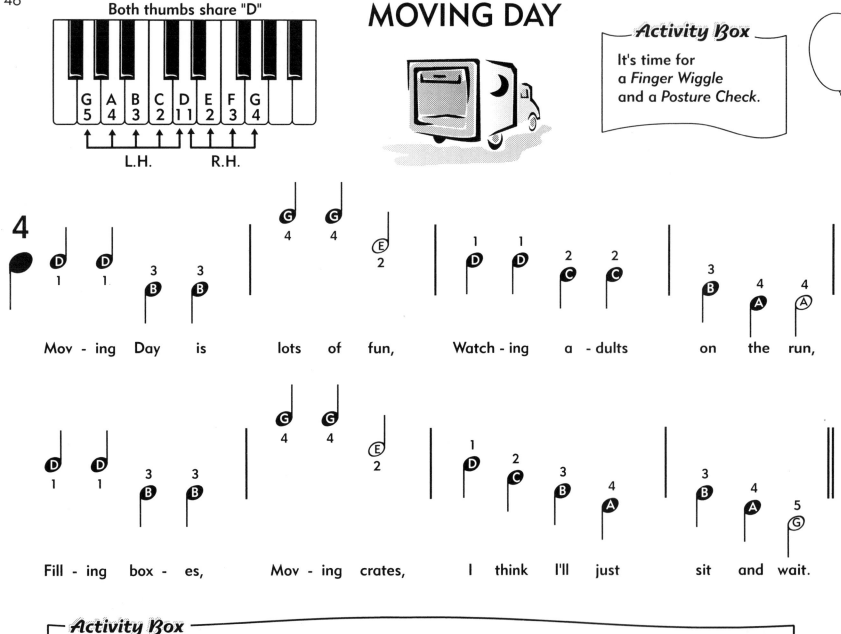

Mov - ing Day is   lots of   fun,   Watch - ing   a - dults   on   the run,

Fill - ing box - es,   Mov - ing crates,   I   think I'll   just   sit   and wait.

Color a
balloon, or
put in a ✓
every time
you do this
page.

Activity Box

Move *Moving Day!* Move your hands so the thumbs share G.
Now play *Moving Day*. Make sure it sounds just like before only higher or lower.

LOOK AND C!

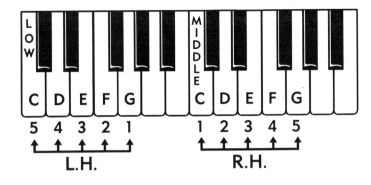

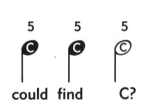

4

C(1) D(2) E(3) F(4)

I just want to

C(1) C(1) C(1)

look and see.

C(5) D(4) E(3) F(2)

If my left hand

C(5) C(5) C(5)

could find C?

G(5) G(5) G(5)

Look at me

C(5) C(5) C(5)

Left's on C

C(1) C(1) C(1) C(1)

Mid - dle C? No!

C(5) C(5) C(5)

Low - er C!

Color in a balloon, or put in a ✓ every time you do this page, (completing 6 times should make you a superstar).

THE STAFF

Music is written on a staff.
The staff is built with 5 lines
and 4 spaces.

Lines

5
4
4
3
3
2
2
1
1

Spaces

Notes may be written on the lines.
The line is in the middle of a line note.

Notes may be written in the spaces.
Space notes fit neatly between the lines.

Activity Box

Draw a circle around the line notes.
Draw a box around the space notes.

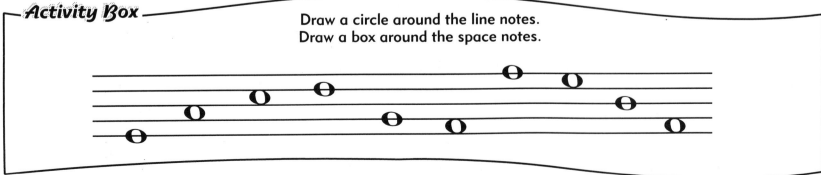

Color a balloon, or put in a ✓ every time you do this page.

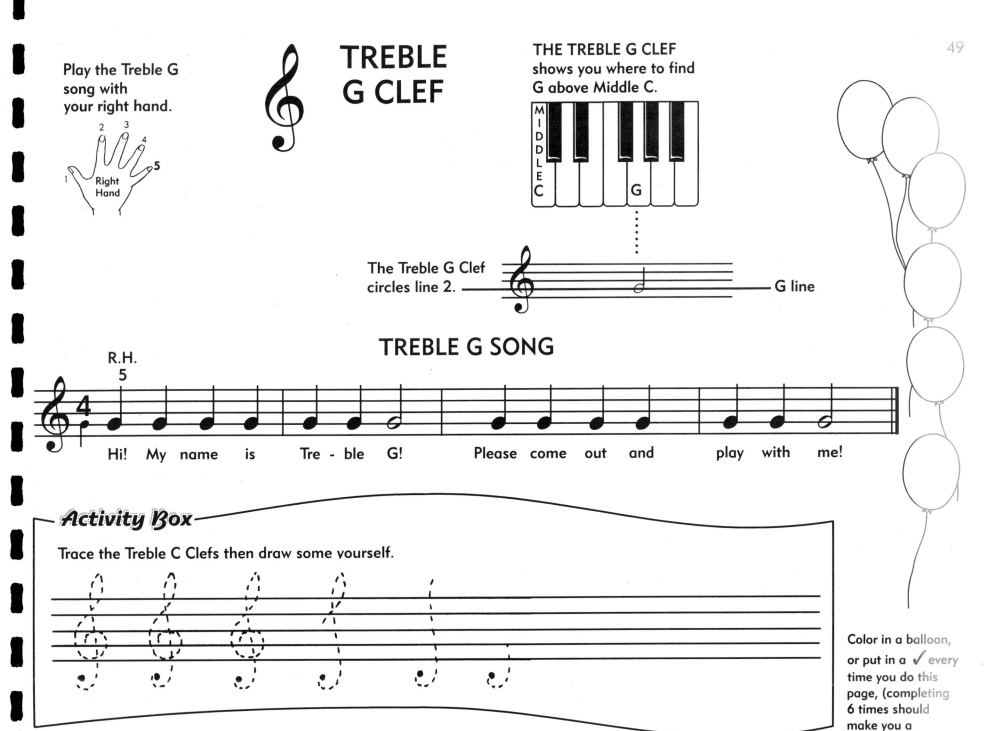

Play the Treble G song with your right hand.

2   3
    4
1   Right   5
    Hand

TREBLE G CLEF

THE TREBLE G CLEF shows you where to find G above Middle C.

MIDDLE C   G

The Treble G Clef circles line 2. ——————— G line

TREBLE G SONG

R.H.
5

Hi! My name is Tre - ble G!   Please come out and   play with me!

Activity Box

Trace the Treble C Clefs then draw some yourself.

Color in a balloon, or put in a ✔ every time you do this page, (completing 6 times should make you a superstar).

MIDDLE C

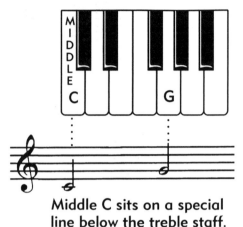

Middle C sits on a special line below the treble staff.

MIDDLE C SONG

Mid - dle   C   Tre - ble   G   I   just   love   this   C   song!

Accompaniment for teacher or advanced student.

Color in a balloon, or put in a ✓ every time you do this page, (completing 6 times should make you a superstar).

ACTIVITY PAGE

On the keyboard below color Middle C red. Color Treble G blue.
Color all of the A's orange, the F's green, the E's yellow and the D's purple,

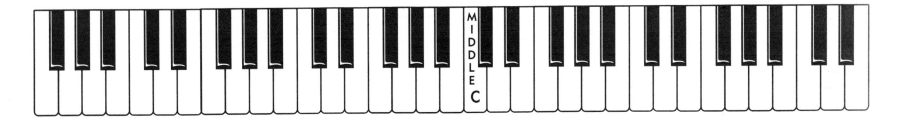

Write the letter C or G below the correct note.

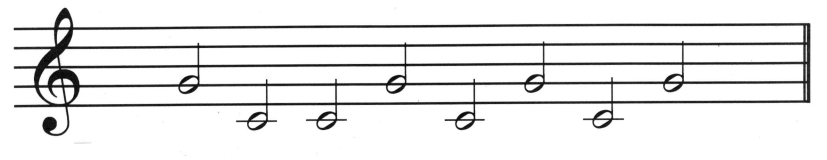

Draw a red circle around the whole notes, a blue circle around the dotted half notes,
a green circle around the half notes and a yellow circle around the quarter notes.

52

BASS CLEF

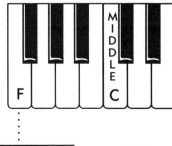

Bass Clef dots are above and below line 4.

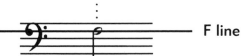

F line

Left Hand

5 4 3 2 1

BASS CLEF F SONG

L.H. 5

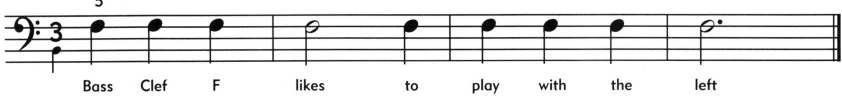

Bass   Clef   F   likes   to   play   with   the   left

Activity Box

Trace the bass clefs, then draw 6 more on the staff.

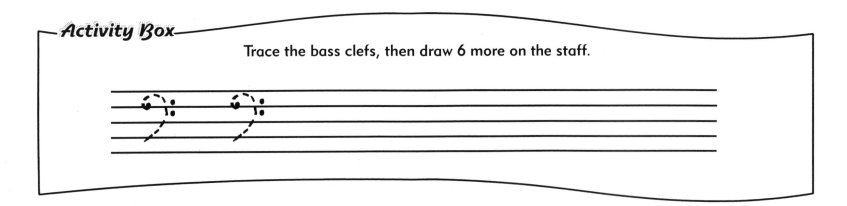

Accompaniment for teacher or advanced student.

Color in a balloon, or put in a ✔ every time you do this page, (completing 6 times should make you a superstar).

BASS CLEF MIDDLE C

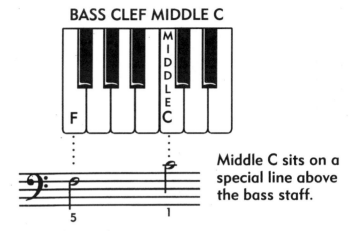

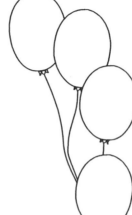

Middle C sits on a special line above the bass staff.

BASS CLEF MIDDLE C

Mid - dle   C   Bass   Clef   F   Thumb   and   ba - by   of   my   left!

Activity Box

Draw a Bass Clef on the staff. Then draw 6 Middle C notes.

Accompaniment for teacher or advanced student.

Color in a balloon, or put in a ✓ every time you play this page, (completing 6 times should make you a superstar).

54

THE GRAND STAFF

The Treble staff and the Bass Staff join together to make the Grand Staff.

The Grand Staff is joined together by a brace.

Middle C

Middle C may be written close to the Treble Clef with the stem turned up. Play this Middle C with the right hand.

When Middle C is written close to the Bass Clef and the stem turned down it is played with the left hand.

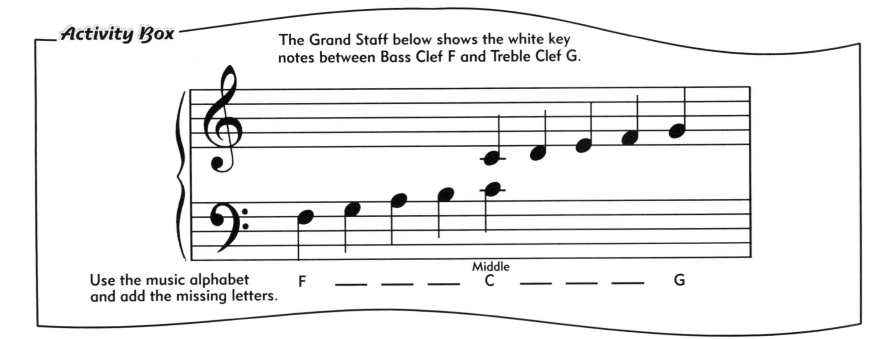

Activity Box

The Grand Staff below shows the white key notes between Bass Clef F and Treble Clef G.

Use the music alphabet and add the missing letters.

F ___ ___ ___ C ___ ___ ___ G

Middle

TWO OLD FRIENDS

Play the Bass Clef notes with your left hand.

Play the Treble Clef notes with your right hand.

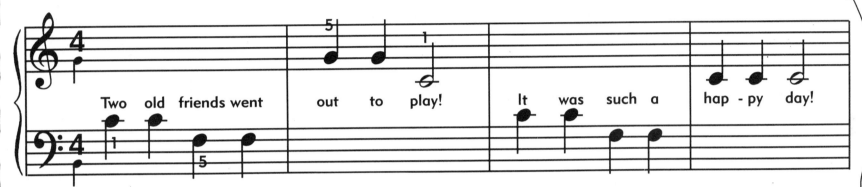

Two old friends went | out to play! | It was such a | hap-py day!

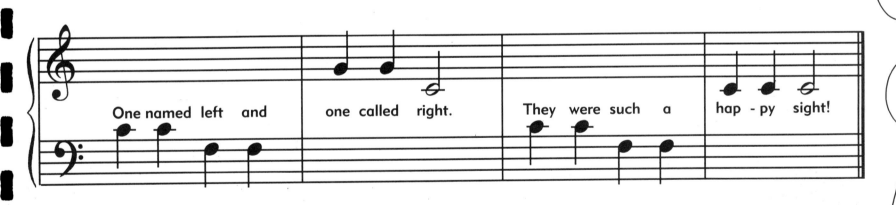

One named left and | one called right. | They were such a | hap-py sight!

Accompaniment for teacher or advanced student.

We hope you have enjoyed learning music from this book.

You are now ready for the Leila Fletcher Piano Course Book 1.

Color in a balloon, or put in a ✓ every time you play this page, (completing 6 times should make you a superstar).

Certificate of Merit~

This certifies that

....

has successfully completed

PRIMER - of the LEILA FLETCHER PIANO COURSE

and is promoted to

BOOK ONE - The LEILA FLETCHER PIANO COURSE

....

TEACHER

Date . . . .